GW01401153

this book

⋛ BELONGS TO ⋛

---

oh.Yes
⋛ WE DiD ⋛™

Ringley? ➡ Replace? (Yes)

Heather @ Tannery
  AGM last night → very positive
  "best in a while"

"Resident" software
- Recharges.
- Savings in contracts (lifts, gates
                window cleaning)
             Insurance

Ringley — £100 bonus for Alex
                2020

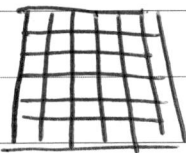

{ Kent

Budget → not accurate

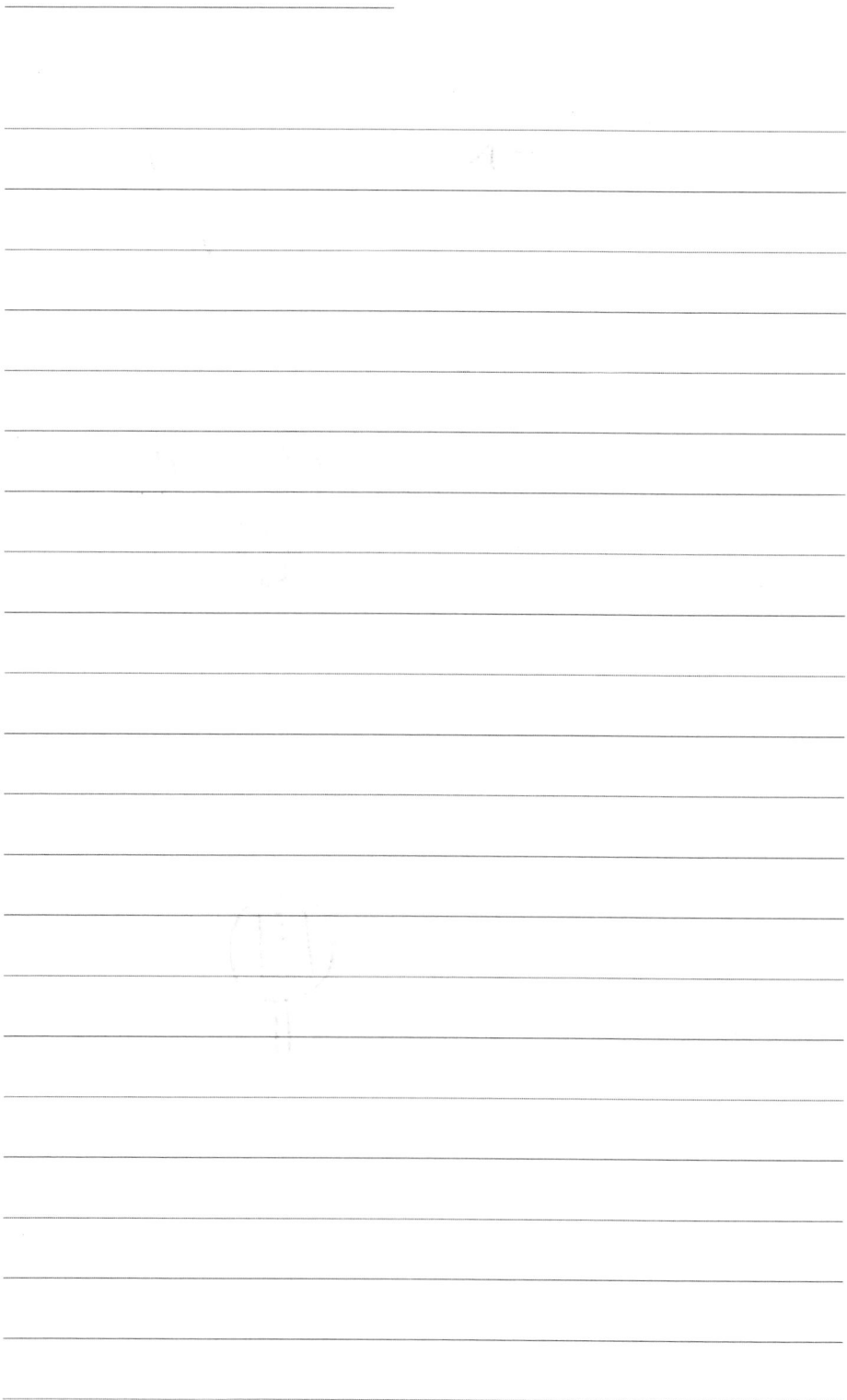

(2021)

10th/11th of April

8th/9th May

12th/13th June

19th/20th June

10th/11th July

17th/18th July

24th/25th July

Kent

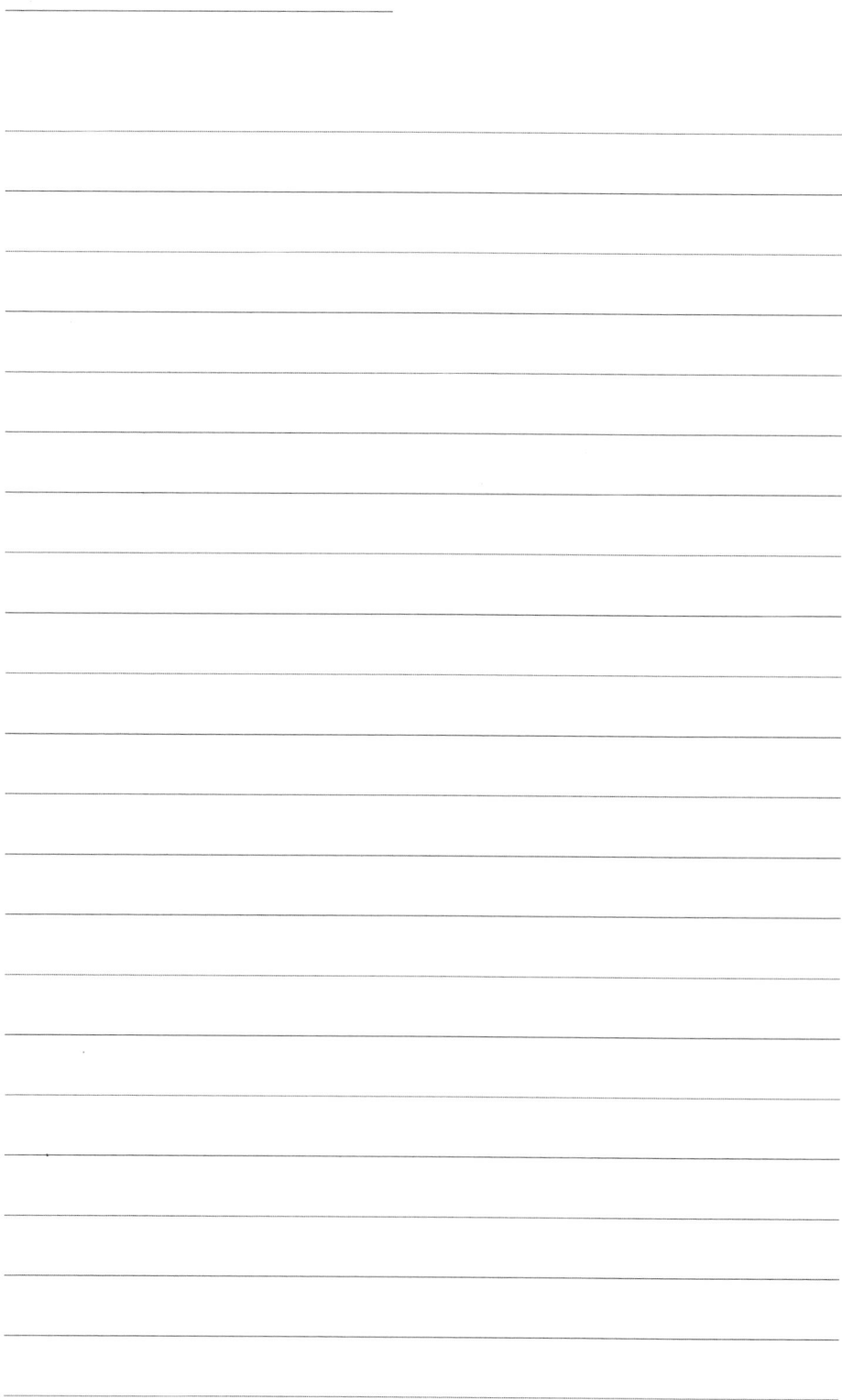

40-64-12

21528005

o 13 payments so far = 5556·72

Final payment Nov 2024

Lloyds MC = 2000
Virgin CC = 6703

Printed in Great Britain
by Amazon